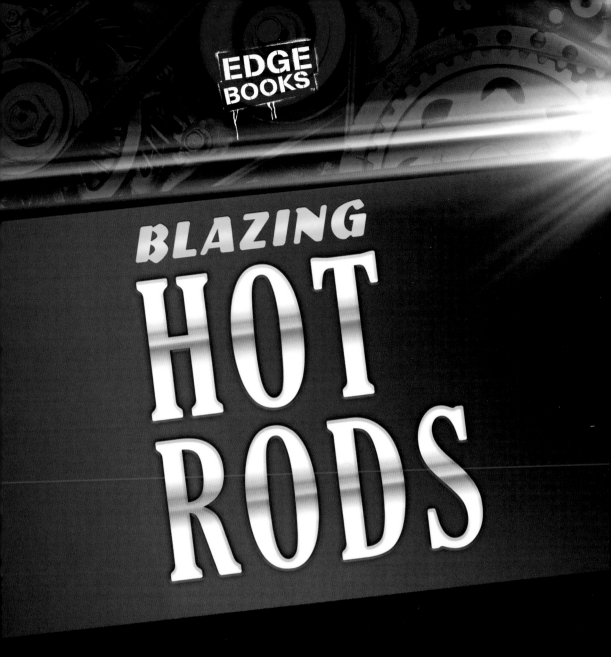

BLAZING
HOT
RODS

by Craig Sodaro

Consultants:
Sammy and Marsha Allen
American Muscle Car Club
Panama City, Florida

CAPSTONE PRESS
a capstone imprint

Edge Books are published by Capstone Press,
1710 Roe Crest Drive, North Mankato, Minnesota 56003
www.capstonepub.com

Library of Congress Cataloging-in-Publication Data
Sodaro, Craig.
Blazing hot rods / by Craig Sodaro.
     pages cm.—(Edge books. Dream cars)
Includes bibliographical references and index.
Summary: "Discusses hot rods, including their history, how they are
built and customized, as well as how hot rod owners enjoy their cars with
shows and races"—Provided by publisher.
Audience: Age 8-14.
Audience: Grades 4 to 6.
ISBN 978-1-4914-2011-9 (library binding)
ISBN 978-1-4914-2182-6 (eBook pdf)
1. Hot rods—Juvenile literature. I. Title.
TL236.3.S663 2015
629.228′6—dc23   2014021516

Editorial Credits
Carrie Braulick Sheely, editor; Heidi Thompson, designer; Pamela J. Mitsakos,
media researcher; Katy LaVigne, production specialist

Photo Credits
Alamy: ©Richard McDowel, 8–9, ©Transcol, 11, ©Tony Watson, 24–25;
CORBIS: ©Bettmann, 7, ©Car Culture, 18, ©Motoring Picture Library, 28–29;
Dreamstime: ©Ananthkrish, cover; Getty Images: Car Culture, 5, The Enthusiast
Network, 12–13; Newscom: ZUMAPRESS/Brian Cah, 23, ZUMAPRESS/Matt
Gdowski, 27; Shutterstock: G. Campbell, 20, Brad Remy, 19, loraks, 15, Steve Mann,
16, Photoraidz, 21

Design Element: Shutterstock: iconizer (throughout), Evgeny Korshenkov

Printed in the United States of America in Stevens Point, Wisconsin
102014   008479WZS15

TABLE OF CONTENTS

AMERICAN CLASSICS

What can you think of that is known for being truly American? You might have thought of apple pie or baseball. But did you also think of hot rods? Hot rods are a true symbol of the American spirit. With owners pouring creativity into their *custom* American-made machines, no two hot rods are exactly alike. You see them in magazines, movies, and artwork. You might have even seen one cruising down the streets. Building one takes time and a lot of work. But to hot rod owners, the results are worth it. The adventure of building a hot rod leads to a blazing-fast car that is truly unique.

The Willys coupe is a popular hot rod. Willys-Overland Motors produced these cars in the early 1940s.

What Makes a Hot Rod?

People don't agree on the exact definition of a hot rod. But most people think of a hot rod as a modified car originally built before the 1950s. The recipe for a hot rod is simple. Find an old car. Cut off some parts to make it lighter. Give it a more powerful engine. Then add finishing touches and paint it so it will turn heads wherever it goes. There are no rules to follow. With some mechanical skill and imagination, anyone can build one.

custom—specially done or made

The Need for Speed

Karl Benz drove the first gas-fueled car in 1886. It had a top speed of 10 miles (16 kilometers) per hour. Early cars were slow and expensive. But that changed when Henry Ford burst onto the car-building scene. Ford sold his first Model T in 1908. Soon after he built car *assembly lines* to make the cars, and the price of his Model Ts dropped. The results? A booming business. It seemed like everybody across the country bought one.

By the 1920s many old Model Ts were abandoned for newer, more advanced cars. Yet the cars were not completely forgotten. Teenagers began buying Model T bodies. They popped new engines into the cars and painted them. Before long the idea of fixing up old cars caught on in more places around the United States.

So why not find out whose hot rod was fastest? Hot rod racing began in California in the early 1920s. Early racers headed out to dry lake beds. As hot rods sped down these lake beds, some of them set land speed records. The car land speed record is the fastest speed that a car has traveled on land. Dry lake beds provide some of the best surfaces for these record attempts.

Assembly-line workers
build a Model T in 1913.

assembly line—an arrangement of workers in a factory; work
passes from one station to the next until the job is done

The Year of Hot Rods

In the story of hot rods, the year 1949 stands out. Many hot rod builders say real hot rodding started that year. Just a year earlier the first hot rod show had been held in Los Angeles, California. The first national speed trials were held in 1949 at the Bonneville Salt Flats in Utah. The common yet dangerous practice of holding street *drag races* led to the opening of the first *commercial* drag strip. It was set up on an abandoned airfield in Santa Ana, California. *Hot Rod Magazine* first appeared in 1949. Hot rods were so popular with teenagers that *Life* magazine stated that hot rod clubs had "sprung up everywhere" in its November 7, 1949, issue.

Early Car Land Speed Records

Year	Driver	Vehicle	Engine Type	Speed (mph)
1899	Count Chasseloup-Laubat	Jeantaud	electric	43.69 (70.3 kph)
1902	Leon Serpollet	Gardner-Serpollet	steam	75.06 (120.8 kph)
1904	Henry Ford	Ford Arrow	gas	91.37 (147 kph)
1904	Louis Rigolly	Gobron-Brillie	gas	103.56 (166.7 kph)
1925	Malcolm Campbell	Sunbeam Bluebird	gas	150.76 (242.6 kph)
1927	Henry Segrave	Sunbeam 1000	gas	203.79 (327.9 kph)
1935	Malcolm Campbell	Railton Rolls-Royce	gas	301.12 (484.6 kph)
1947	John Cobb	Railton Mobil Special	gas	394.19 (634.4 kph)

Fact

The Santa Ana drag strip was complete with electronic timers. The timers helped make it popular with racers.

drag race—a contest in which people race two cars over a short distance

commercial—to do with buying and selling things

A HOT ROD FOR EVERYONE

Hot rods fall into different categories. The oldest is the roadster. Roadsters don't have roofs or side windows. The rear body is often hacked off. Early roadsters didn't even have windshields, headlights, or fenders. Some even had their doors removed. What they did have was a souped-up engine that could help the cars pick up speed quickly to win races. Hot rod builders view the 1932 Ford Roadster with a V-8 engine as the classic roadster.

Fact

Clarence "Chili" Catallo built a classic hot rod when he bought a 1932 Ford coupe for $75. The Beach Boys put a picture of the bright blue car on their 1963 hit album *Little Deuce Coupe*.

Little Deuce Coupes

A car with a permanently attached roof and two doors is called a coupe. Coupes can be turned into hot rods too. Coupes aren't stripped down like roadsters. All safety features remain on the car. But hot rodders make other changes. Some hot rod coupes have extra long front ends to house bigger engines. Sometimes there's no front hood, so the engine is exposed. Wide tires and flashy radiator grilles add style.

The 1932 Ford coupe (right) is popular with hot rod enthusiasts.

Works of Art

Every hot rod builder is an artist. Each one customizes a car to make it a unique machine. Replacing the original engine with a more powerful one is a common starting point. A builder may lower the body or remove the roof and back seats to lighten the car. For finishing touches many builders add new grilles and extra chrome for dazzle. They may cover the seats in leather or replace the car's carpets. Other builders skip the dazzle altogether. They create "rat rods." These hot rods are built from a variety of old parts. Often the parts are from several car models. Rat rod bodies are usually left completely unpainted. Wondering how to spot one? Look for a rusty hot rod!

PRIVATE
NO PARK
AT ANY

Some hot rodders have built really unusual vehicles. The bodies of "belly tank" hot rods came from fuel tanks attached to World War II (1939-1945) airplanes. They looked like bullets on wheels. People first built these hot rods right after the war. But the cars still pop up at car shows and in museums.

A "streamliner" looks almost like a space rocket on wheels. It has one seat with a long body. The body covers at least two wheels almost to the ground. Because they're so sleek, streamliners have set world speed records. Their *aerodynamic* shape reduces *drag*, which helps them cut through the air.

Hot rodders sometimes left their belly tank hot rods unpainted.

aerodynamic—built to move easily through the air
drag—the force created when air strikes a moving object; drag slows down moving objects

BUILDING A HOT ROD

Building a hot rod can be a big challenge. It takes money, skill, and a lot of patience, but it's worth it! What does a hot rod builder need to get started? A strong background in mechanics and welding is crucial. Equipment and tool needs will vary from day to day. Hot rodders who don't own their own tools often work in auto shops after hours. They also may rent space with other hot rodders who share equipment.

The first step is to draw a plan for the hot rod. A builder can take the design as far as budget, skill, and imagination will allow.

Once there's a plan, the hot rodder needs a frame. Usually the frame comes from an old car that doesn't run anymore. A search through a junkyard can turn up the perfect frame. Builders without a lot of experience usually choose a frame and body combination. They will then have the sides of the car to work with as well as the frame. Building the sides, rear, and front panels of a car takes a lot of work.

Welding uses heat to join metal pieces together.

A supercharger can boost engine power.

Hot Rod Horsepower

One of the most important parts of a hot rod is the engine. Every hot rodder wants one with big *horsepower*. Many builders buy new engines for their cars. Some hot rodders buy old engines and rebuild them to save money.

It's important that the new engine fits into the hot rod being built. If a hot rodder is going to "go big" with a car, a 1965 to 1971 Chevy Big-Block V-8 might be a good choice. *Hot Rod Magazine* readers voted it the second most popular engine of all time. If the hot rod is going to be smaller, a 1955 to 2003 Chevy Small-Block V-8 is a good choice. It's called "the universal soldier" of hot rodding. This engine was produced in great numbers, and it is affordable for most builders.

For even more power, a builder can add a supercharger or a turbocharger. Both parts do the same thing. They *compress* air so more of it is pushed into the *cylinders*. More fuel can then be pumped in, and each explosion is bigger. The difference between a supercharger and a turbocharger is the power supply. A belt connected to the engine runs a supercharger. The turbocharger gets its power from the exhaust system.

horsepower—a unit for measuring an engine's power
compress—to press or squeeze something so that it
    will fit into a small space
cylinder—a hollow area inside an engine in which
    fuel burns to create power

Beyond the Engine

Even with the engine in place, a hot rod builder still has a great deal of work left. Brakes need to be installed. Most modern hot rods have disc brakes. These brakes have more stopping power than drum brakes.

A builder needs to decide how high or low the car will ride. To adjust this feature the builder changes the *suspension* of the car. The builder needs to weigh the advantages and disadvantages of these adjustments. Lowering the suspension makes the car easier to drive and faster because it's more aerodynamic. The downside is that tires wear more unevenly. The car can also hit the ground or objects more easily, causing damage.

A hot rod may have a leaf-spring or a coil-spring suspension. A leaf-spring suspension is made up of several long, flexible metal pieces. The pieces are bundled together and attached to the rear *axle* near each wheel. A coil-spring suspension uses metal coils. If the car has leaf springs, a builder can de-arch them to lower the suspension. To raise it the builder can increase the arch. If the car has coil springs, the builder can lower the suspension by cutting the springs. To raise this suspension, a builder can use coil spring spacers.

Many hot rodders lower their cars' suspensions.

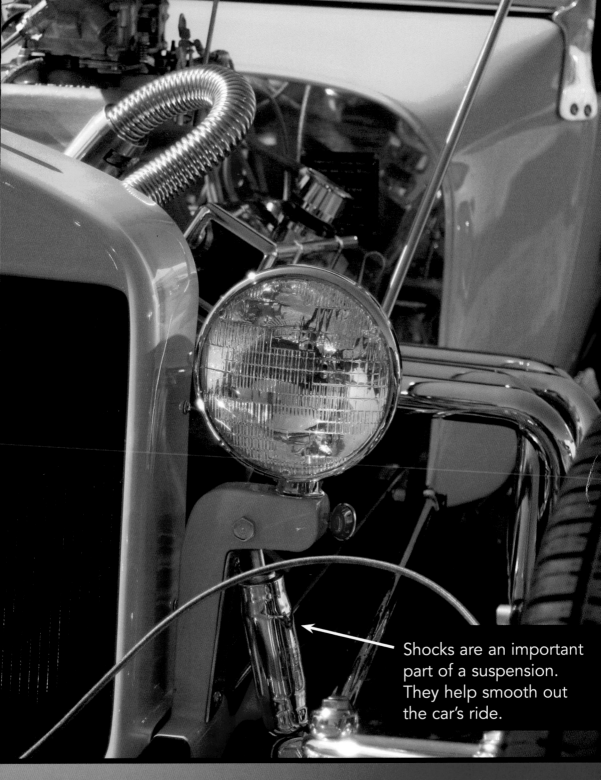

Shocks are an important part of a suspension. They help smooth out the car's ride.

suspension—the system of springs and shock absorbers that absorbs a car's up-and-down movements

axle—a rod attached to the middle of a wheel on a vehicle

Flame paint jobs are common on hot rods.

Fact

Hot rodder Ed "Big Daddy" Roth created the popular "Rat Fink" cartoon character. It came to symbolize the hot rod-building craze in California during the 1960s.

Details, Details

Wiring is one of the last jobs of building a hot rod. The ignition, lights, and dashboard all need to be wired.

Choosing exhaust pipes is a big decision for builders too. Many hot rodders choose chrome exhaust pipes. Builders also look for pipes that will give them just the right sound. The

an exhaust pipe being installed

classic, muffled roar that comes with a stomp on the gas pedal is perfect for many hot rodders.

Fenders, running boards, and radiator grilles finish off the exterior of the car. Many builders try to keep the classic look of the car. If the original car had running boards, the hot rodder will usually add them.

Art on Wheels

Painting a hot rod is the final step. First a builder sands the body carefully with an electric sander to smooth and clean the entire surface. Everything the builder doesn't want painted is covered. If the body already has paint on it, the car is sprayed with a sealer so that color won't bleed through. Then the hot rodder sprays on a primer, which helps the paint stick to the surface. The paint is sprayed on last. Some builders choose paint with a matte finish. For shine the builder may choose a metallic paint or one with a glossy finish. Many hot rodders paint flames on their cars. Some hot rodders even paint on fancy lettering or pictures.

HOT RODS IN THE SPOTLIGHT

Horsepower and hot rods go hand in hand. It's only natural for hot rodders to want their cars to not only go fast, but faster than others. The popularity of hot rods led to paved racetracks being built in every U.S. state and around the world. The National Hot Rod Association (NHRA) has been a driving force in building racetracks in the United States.

Early hot rod races were drag races, and these are still a favorite of hot rodders. Most drag strips are either 1/4 mile (0.4 km) or 1/8 mile (0.2 km) long.

Other racetracks are mainly oval but also include a straightaway. These tracks host classic hot rod races along with other types of races.

At the Bonneville Salt Flats in western Utah, hot rodders race on a flat dried-up salt water lake bed. Many vehicle world speed records have been set there. Each year Speed Week draws hundreds of hot rodders and thousands of spectators to Bonneville.

Popular U.S. Racetracks

Track	City	Year Built	Track Type	Capacity
Pomona Raceway	Pomona, CA	1934	oval	40,000
Bandimere Speedway	Denver, CO	1958	¼-mile (0.4-km) drag strip	28,500
Gainesville Raceway	Gainesville, FL	1969	¼-mile drag strip; road course for vehicle testing and driver training	36,000
Las Vegas Motor Speedway	Las Vegas, NV	1971	oval superspeedway 2.5-mile (4-km) road course; ¼-mile drag strip; dirt oval	131,000
Houston Motorsports Park	Houston, TX	1979	⅛-mile (0.2-km) drag strip; ⅜-mile (0.6-km) oval	30,000

Streamliners get set to race during Speed Week in 2011.

Catch Me If You Can!

What does a classic hot rod drag race look like? Two hot rods move to the starting line. When given the signal, they roar down the drag strip. The first hot rod to reach the finish line wins. This style of racing is called heads-up.

Bracket racing is another drag race style. A driver tells the officials how long it will take the car to reach the finish line. This driver is in competition with another driver who chose a time in the same time *bracket*. Whoever gets to the finish line first wins—as long as he or she reached the chosen time. If the driver is under that time, it's a loss.

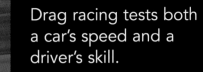

Drag racing tests both a car's speed and a driver's skill.

Each year the NHRA sponsors the famous Mello Yello Drag Racing Series. The races are usually three-day events. Participation in many races is open to any driver. Usually the 16 fastest cars compete in the finals in a two-vehicle elimination tournament. Eventually, only two cars are left. The winner of the last race takes home the prize.

Fact

In official drag races, a set of lights called a "Christmas tree" signals drivers to start. Drivers pull up to the line on red, get ready to go on yellow, and screech off on the green light.

bracket—a category

Lights! Cameras! Hot Rods!

From the birth of hot rodding in the 1920s, hot rods have had starring roles in movies. A classic 1932 Ford five-window hot rod stole the spotlight in George Lucas' *American Graffiti.*

Plenty of songs about hot rods have topped the charts too. "Drag Race" by Don Pearly and "Hot Rod Baby" by Rocky Davis are just a couple songs celebrating hot rods.

Showing Off

Hot rodders love to show off their cars. That's why there are hundreds of hot rod shows every year. Thousands of car lovers show up to get an eyeful of the most amazing and original cars ever built. If you go to one, you might see the Clapton Vicky, a 1932 Ford custom four-door Ford. Maybe you could catch a glimpse of the band ZZ Top's Eliminator Coupe. This bright red hot rod was built from a 1933 Ford Coupe.

Hot rods line up at a show in Las Vegas, Nevada.

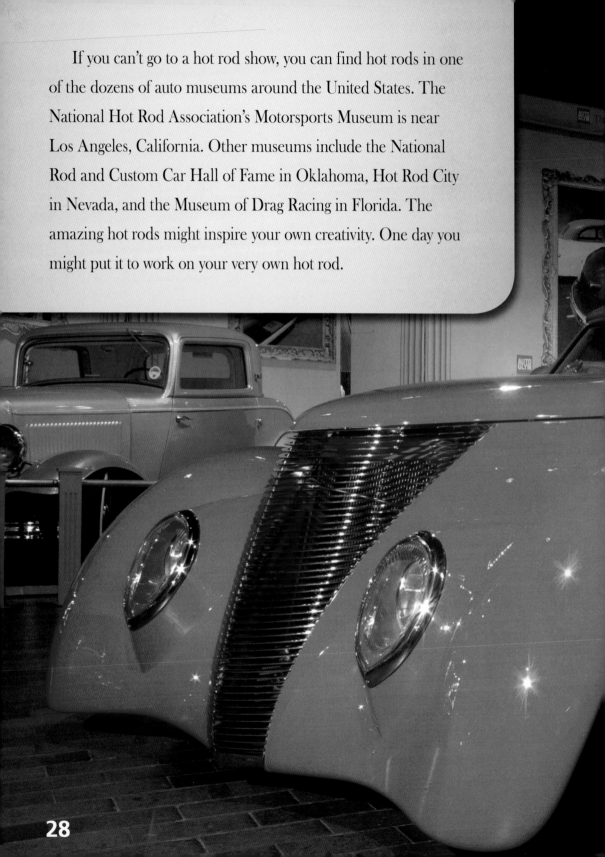

If you can't go to a hot rod show, you can find hot rods in one of the dozens of auto museums around the United States. The National Hot Rod Association's Motorsports Museum is near Los Angeles, California. Other museums include the National Rod and Custom Car Hall of Fame in Oklahoma, Hot Rod City in Nevada, and the Museum of Drag Racing in Florida. The amazing hot rods might inspire your own creativity. One day you might put it to work on your very own hot rod.

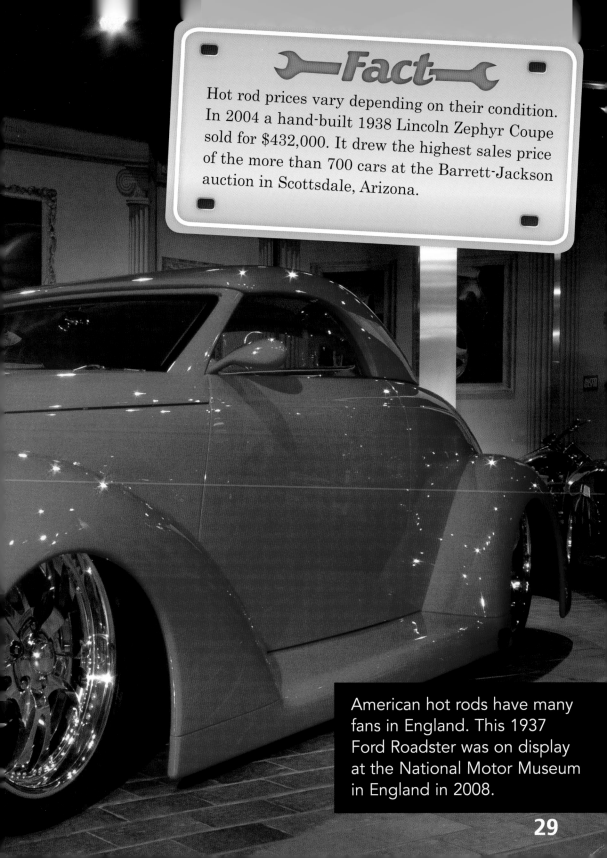

Hot rod prices vary depending on their condition. In 2004 a hand-built 1938 Lincoln Zephyr Coupe sold for $432,000. It drew the highest sales price of the more than 700 cars at the Barrett-Jackson auction in Scottsdale, Arizona.

American hot rods have many fans in England. This 1937 Ford Roadster was on display at the National Motor Museum in England in 2008.

GLOSSARY

aerodynamic (air-oh-dye-NA-mik)—built to move easily through the air

assembly line (uh-SEM-blee LYN)—an arrangement of workers in a factory; work passes from one station to the next until the job is done

axle (AK-suhl)—a rod attached to the middle of a wheel on a vehicle

bracket (BRAK-it)—a category

budget (BUH-juht)—a plan for spending money

commercial (kuh-MUHR-shuhl)—to do with buying and selling things

compress (kuhm-PRES)—to press or squeeze something so that it will fit into a small space

coupe (KOOP)—a car with a fixed roof and usually two doors

custom (KUHS-tuhm)—specially done or made

cylinder (SI-luhn-duhr)—a hollow area inside an engine in which fuel burns to create power

drag (DRAG)—the force created when air strikes a moving object; drag slows down moving objects

drag race (DRAG RAYSS)—a race in which two cars begin at a standstill and drive in a straight line at high speeds for a short distance

drag strip (DRAG STRIP)—a short straight track on which a drag race is run

frame (FRAYM)—the rigid main support structure for the body of a car

horsepower (HORSS-pou-ur)—a unit for measuring an engine's power

roadster (ROHD-stur)—an open or roofless car that usually seats two people; some roadsters have a fabric top that folds back

superspeedway (soo-pur-SPEED-way)—a large oval racetrack that is more than 1.5 miles (2.4 kilometers) long

suspension (suh-SPEN-shuhn)—the system of springs and shock absorbers that absorbs a car's up-and-down movements

READ MORE

Brush, Jim. *Custom Cars*. Fast Facts. Mankato, Minn.: Sea-to-Sea Publications, 2012.

Gifford, Clive. *Car Crazy*. New York: DK Publishing, 2012.

Kenny, Karen Latchana. *The Science of Car Racing*. The Science of Speed. North Mankato, Minn.: Capstone, 2014.

Sandler, Michael. *Hot Hot Rods*. Fast Rides. New York: Bearport Pub., 2011.

INTERNET SITES

FactHound offers a safe, fun way to find Internet sites related to this book. All of the sites on FactHound have been researched by our staff.

Here's all you do:

Visit *www.facthound.com*

Type in this code: 9781491420119

 Check out projects, games and lots more at **www.capstonekids.com**

INDEX